E
Evincepub
Publishing

Evincepub Publishing

Parijat Extension, Bilaspur, Chhattisgarh 495001
First Published By Evincepub Publishing 2021

ISBN: 978-93-5446-017-3

$E=mc^2$

(Poetic Explanation of Einstein's Theory of Relativity)

By

BUSHRA NIDA

*Dedicated to my dear Dad who can't take this book
in hand as he resides wherefrom no one returns!
And to all the passionate lovers of science*

ABOUT THE AUTHOR

Bushra Nida is 12th class student. She hails from Nasirabad (Kanipora) village of Kulgam, Kashmir. She has written 2 books so far. Her book *TULIPS OF FEELINGS* is her maiden poetry book that got Appreciation Award from **India Book Of Records.** Her second book THE DAVY (Poetic rendition of Elements of Periodic Table) gained international applause and is registered in **Golden Book of World Records** and **Asia Book Of Records.** She won **International Kalam's Golden Award 2021** for her second book. A famous writer from Ayodhya named Mrigendra Raj Pandey was so impressed by the achievement of Bushra Nida that he wrote the biography of Bushra Nida titled *Siraj-e- Kashmir* in Hindi.

Bushra Nida is very ambitious about her contribution to scientific knowledge. This book is her 3rd publication. She lives with her mother and an elder sister.

PREFACE

If you have always wondered and never really understood the depth of Einstein's earth-shattering equation, or if you wish to elaborate that equation in more plain words and analysis, then this is the book.

I painted the theory of relativity through a canvas of pen and paper I have framed Einstein's life and his famous equation in beautiful verses. Further, my take on his dogma regarding the equation could be understood well in simple words.

I have tried to explain how the sun and other stars in the universe works, how matter can become energy and vice-versa, radioactivity, radiocarbon phenomenon, CT scans, PET technique (Positron emission topography Scans), telecommunications, how $E=mc^2$ makes the technique possible and I have put an effort to explain about black holes, Big Bang many more Important implications' associated with it.

"Science without religion is lame, religion without science is blind." says Albert Einstein. So no genius can restrict the logic to science only, its religion that tends to us provide hints for our mental-broadening, which later become the root cause of our scientific temper. There are many other causes as well to be a religious fundamentalist to chop the metal of science, the miracles have there been a base for various hypotheses, phenomena and various discoveries cum inventions.

I have illustrated the mutual interdependence of religion and science. I have quoted how the Vedas, the Quran, the Bible support this equation. I have done comparative research on the holy books and then came jot this book, yes I have written that in the poetic medium.

"Any fool can know, the point is to understand"
Albert Einstein

I have compiled a few examples that would clear or complete the idea.

The book can prove to be helpful for students as the beautifully written verses embedded with the equation 'E=mc^2' can stay longer in their minds.

Bushra Nida

ADVANCE PRAISES FOR THE BOOK

A young kid with brains gives out her understanding of Einstein and his famous equation, in verses. Scientists, specifically those belonging to discipline of Physics, have attempted the same for the last hundred years, with varying degrees of success. It, however, can't be claimed that her assertions are all correct, particularly when she relates theological and mystical phenomenon to the theory of relativity. However, what is to be appreciated is the level of thoughts and effort put in to think above average in trying to decode the $E=mc^2$ equation. If for nothing else, the child needs to be encouraged and provided stimulus to enlarge her thinking and achieve better results in future. I wish her well for her forays in the world of science thinkers in the forthcoming ventures.

Hilal Ahmad Bakshi
Associate Professor
Govt Degree College, Pampore

Well, considering Post-postmodernism no poetry is lesser and its soul lies in its depth, profound works catch more eyes with perfection in devices of poetry within the ambit of figurative language. We went through many distinct periods of literature, then only we surpass here, reverberate musings in extensive style. But then the beauty of art lies in attracting the eyes of readers, literature lovers and fit-in various stages, asked by the time from revolutions to gatherings, every home's melody. In this regard, we were from time to time showered with inks, thoughts and sayings of literary-giants. None among us reaps results without getting ushered from the intellect of those spiritually connected saints of literature.

When it comes to our Kashmir valley, never did we abandon the journey, our presence always provided the utmost fragrance. Kashmiri, Urdu, Hindi, Sanskrit and English, in every aspect, we asserted our metal before the world from times immemorial. We always served literature from Laleshwari, Mehjuur, Habba Khatoon, Amin Kamil, Abdul Ahad Azad, Aga Shahid Ali, ZindaKaul to the present-day poets.

Bushra Nida compiled her thoughts, after-thoughts, and ideas and summed her knowledge to surprise our intelligence. For a children writer rhyme, rhythm, consonance, alliteration matters more, to give a moral, ethical lesson among the children. The stage of complexity would then depend on, understanding the field and exercising one's class, art and experience. This experience if not that extensive, won't defunct the ideas put into words by a writer or a poet hence, for no saint is an angel and no great poet a perfectionist from the very beginning. By the way, the idea must be valued provided the fact poetry provides less freedom, and ought to have certain gulps of structural idea beneath heaps of intelligence.

In times of conflict, if an optimistic and encouraging face of society comes forward, why to turn our heads from it. Neither we creep towards it and seldom spread the message, nor we get mistaken which eventually lead to the death of art within the artist. I, therefore, harness on the constructive ideology and promise to gallop the lineage of amateurish devotees who have the potential to turn into the crown of the valley. Bushra Nida's collection gives us a substantial amount of ideas placed rhythmically, and in a beautiful style. Science's well-known genius 'Albert Einstein' pressed more on the same terms, where Bushra could win the marathon.

I congratulate her on her blissfully writing a book 'E=MC^2. Her fantasy has no limits but her caricature of ideas will massively lead her in this aspect of life and literature.

Zakir Malik
Budding writer

Writing is quite hard, even for the ones who write all the time. It is increasingly very hard to portray equations of Einstein through the canvas of poetry. Well, I still can't believe that I came through such a budding writer who in her first book left everyone astonished, and the second one will be definitely an alluring and informative for all the readers. The way the author has framed the Einstein's equation in a beautiful verse makes the reader keen to go through the book. The way the author has painted the theory of relativity through the canvas of pen and paper is quite fantastic and wonderful. The most marvelous part of the book is the way she interprets the spirituality of the Prophet, and touches the mystical belief and relates all of them with a wonderful equation of relativity.

"The E=mc^2 "beautifully written by "Bushra Nida" is worth reading and the author should be highly appreciated for such a fantastic work. This book can prove to be helpful for students as the beautifully written verses embedded with the equation " E= mc^2 can stay longer in their minds. I highly appreciate the author and feel scarcity of words to praise her work. I assure all the readers that this book will be quite helpful and joyous.

I wish that the author gives us more exciting writings in future and hope she becomes one of the most renowned writers in the world.

Syed Aksa Andrabi
Budding Writer

Bushra Nida, a young kid & a prominent writer, takes what could have been a dull recitation of the facts surrounding Albert Einstein's famous theory of relativity and transforms it into a surprising and compelling poetry book.

If you've always wondered, and never really understood, the meaning of Einstein's earth-shattering equation, this is the book. Separately explain each component of the equation: E for energy, = for the equals sign, m for mass, C for celeritas (Latin for swift, as Einstein dubbed the speed of light) a number by squaring it.

In this very book, the poetess has mentioned Shab-e-Meraj (Night Ascension). And she wants to tell us that theory of relativity can explain Lailatul Meraj. In brief, $E=mc^2$ responds positively to the question of 'how does a human being can go a thousand year distance within a couple of minutes.' Theory of general relativity also foresaw the Big Bang event, and predicted that time is slowed down when the attraction is intense. This means that the watch of a man in space and of a man on the ground shows different times, because since the man on the ground is strongly affected by the Earth's gravity, his watch is slower compared to the watch on the man in space. One can interpret it in terms of Mehraj performed by Prophet Muhammad (pbuh) where science & religion can be reconciled.

There are many ways to do away with wandering thoughts, striking the mind regularly. Some may simplify the intuition, propensity towards the line of reasoning. Yet many of the intellectuals come up with different mediums and pour the underlying understanding into their way to offer then to the world in general. It's never easy to plan such kind of reflections and place outside before the readers to digest or to lend their suggestions afterwards.

'This book' is the containment of her understanding towards $E=MC^2$, though to compose her perception in verses seems awkward but she rather loves to go through the same in the morning as well as in dusk of her regular days. She might have stricken with a lot of verses without forcing her nerves to do so.

In nutshell, it shows how this famous equation changed the world irrevocably. Guys, It's a highly readable book about a complex topic, and you won't need a science degree to understand and enjoy it.

And I would like my readers to examine the verses, and prepare a well-defined analysis that can guide her thoughts hereafter.

Imtiyaz Gull
Budding Writer

$$E=mc^2$$

$E=mc^2$

The brain-wider than sky
God's truth, no lie.

The brain deeper than sea
Genius hits a target that no one can see.

Brain equal to weight of God
Equal to pounds and pounds.

He was a man beyond limits with mixture of
madness.
His View was complex

He was genius
But his equation $E=mc^2$ was ingenious.

Had an IQ of about 160
Truly Flashy

He was neither learned nor acquired
He was an oracle, accomplished.

He was a man, with complete brain
That could ran faster than any train.

The man who became synonymous to brilliance,
Smartest person who ever lived in the universe.

He was a polymath
As scare as hen's teeth.

He was a rose in a world full of daisies
Garden was in his eyes where grow roses and white

E=mc2

lilies

The fragrance of his mind Sanctifies air and fills
night
He was the flower of light.

He was a gifted genius, Newtonian spoiler
Physicist and Nobel Prize Winner.

He was an old soul, with young eyes and beautiful
heart
Known all over in the world, he was enough smart

His brilliance took him to the stars
He lived a worthwhile life coz he lived for others.

You are extraordinary like the terrain in the sky of
delight
 Swept away the darkest rays and bought light.

He was agape intellect
The only human with no secret
He was a sea of conscious reasoning
He was brainiac

Whose formulas and theory
Advanced the Scientific community

In the nuclear weaponry
And changed the whole destiny.

Your talent is a gift
Your skill is prize

You are a blessing
Your mind - your reward.

Yes talking of Great Albert Einstein
Born on 14 March, 1879.

In Ulm, Wurttemberg, Germany
Grew up in a secular Jewish family.

First child born to Herman and Pauline
Was stupendous Einstein.

His parents were secular middle class Jews
The Einstein's were non- observant Ashkenazi Jews.

He attended school as a young boy Took studies as
Joy.

Received instructions at home on Judaism and violin
Was passionate to become Musician

By the age of 12, he had taught himself geometry
Thought he would be good because he could think
mathematically.

At the age of 16, he failed to qualify to train as
electric engineer And decided to study math and
physics to become a teacher.

He learned to speak at a very late age
Uncommon, learned violin but not earned money for
the same.

E=mc2

His head was big, but still
And he didn't know how to hold a Pencil.

One year after Einstein was born around 18th
centaury
His parents moved to Munich to establish
engineering company.

Einstein's childhood, was normal except his family
irritation
In 1884, to get prepared for School, he received pvt
Education.

The secondary school he attended was later named
after him
The Albert Einstein Gymnasium

He wrote his first scientific paper
As a teenager

One thing you probably didn't know about Einstein
He was renounced his German Citizenship at 16.

Most influential Physicist
Was Dyslexic
Albert was inquisitive and rebel
He was Dyslexic and disliked Grammar.

Eisenstein's family is the family of renowned
physicists.
He personally loves science and mathematics.

E=mc2

He was a strict vegetarian
He was a bohemian.

Albert was interesting guy
Indisputably smart and reputedly shy.

His legacy statistical
But had been more egoistical.

Einstein the fizzy haired
Proved E=mc Squared.

The great Einstein
Loved wine

And after sipping a little
He would play upon his fiddle

We hail Albert Einstein's Creativity
For his grand 'Tour de force and relativity

Brilliant, smart and wise
The son of Herman Einstein.

His teachers thought his abilities limited
And see his brain was later exhibited
Remains a tough climb
To imagine space time.

Albert Einstein
Expanded our view beyond skyline.

He fancied
A hairstyle much to be desired,

He invested a lifetime on science and discovery
Shared his knowledge and philosophy

World changed by his knowledge and theory
Mostly the General theory of relativity

Justly famous for devising his theory
Of Relativity

He was a German-born Scientist
Worked on theoretical physics

Einstein being Jewish ethnicity
Didn't return to Germany

Due to Hitler's anti-Semitic policies
Country was ruled by Nazis

His family was Jewish
But not very religious

Later became very interested in Judaism
Politically active for socialism and Zionism

He apparently did not like School
And teachers considered him as fool

When he was 5, his father bought him compass
Showed he had a great mind for maths and science.

E=mc2

When he was a teen
Around 15

He with his family
 Moved to Milan in Italy.

When his grandmother saw Einstein
For the first time,

Cried out loud: much too thick, much too thick.
And thought he was sick.

He learned a lot about science from his dad
Didn't finish school in Germany but ended up in
Switzerland

Albert immigrated to US in 1933
He was fleeing from the Nazis in Germany.

Considered as the most influential Physicist of 20th
Centaury
His father was a salesman later ran to
electrochemical factory.

He had a sister Maria, so slim
Two years younger to him

In 1903, he married Mileva Maric
Physics student whom he met in Zurich.

Who was Mileva Maric?
Only female student at Zurich polytechnic

E=mc2

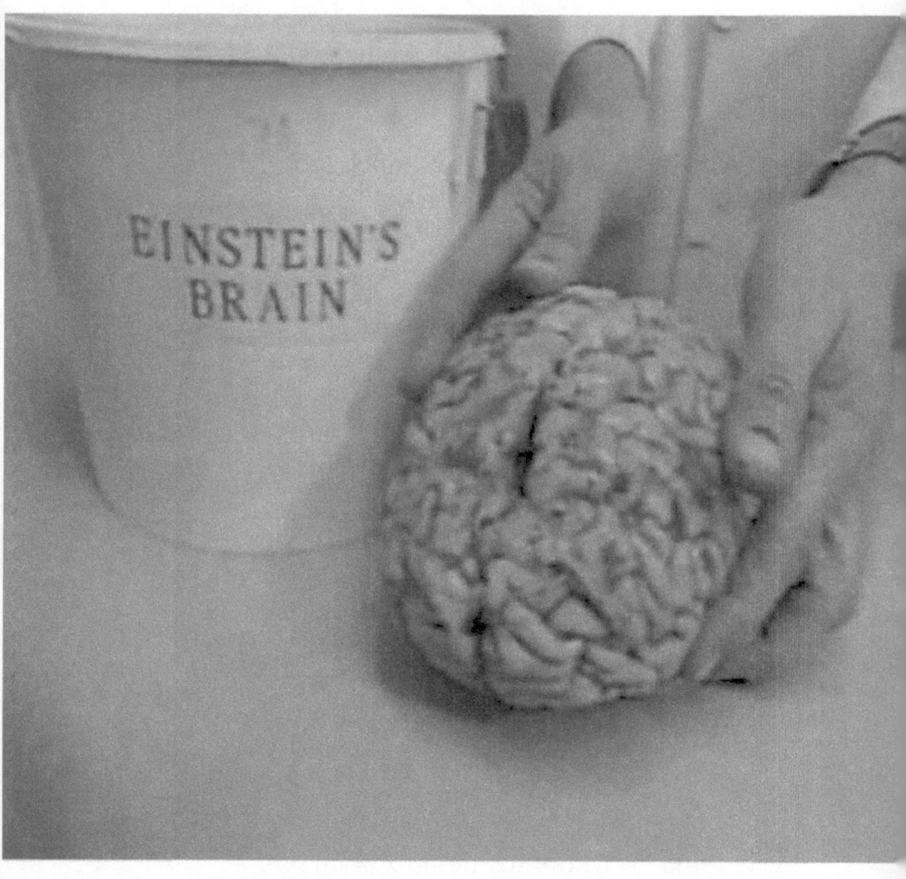

They had 3- children
Two sons and a daughter.

Hans, Edward and daughter Leiserl
Had begun an affair with his cousin Lowenthal.

Einstein had a massive influence on contemporary
Physics
Bought into existence Quantum mechanics.

A great genius Eisenstein
Loved to drink wine

Physicist Einstein
Redesigned his hairline

He enjoyed the notoriety
Having theorized relativity.

He published books and articles in tons
More than 300 scientific papers and 150 non-
scientific ones.

Proposed quantum theory
Explained evidence for atomic theory

Reconciled 'Maxwell's equation for electricity
And equivalence of mass and energy.

Discredited the concept of lumniferous ether
Amalen der Physik Albert's first paper

E=mc2

It was published in 1901
With title Folgerungenaus den
Capillaritätserscheinungen

Einstein returned to the problem
Of thermodynamic fluctuation

In 1916, he predicted gravitational waves.
Produced wormhole model called 'Eisenstein Rosen
bridges.

Modification of concept of Torsion
Was made by Einstein and Cartan.

His 'Einstein field equation describe how space
curves
The geodesic equation describes how particle moves.

He showed us the wave particle duality
Gloriously in 19th century.
Introduced idea of zero point energy
In his second quantum theory

He proposed the possibility of Stimulated emission
The physical process that makes possible, maser and
laser

Discovered Louis de Broglie's
Work and supported his ideas

And gave wave Equation for
De Broglie waves

E=mc2

Sup. frontal s.
Mid. frontal s.
Inf. frontal s.
Precentral s.
Central s.
Post central s.
Intraparietal s.
Sup. frontal s.
Middle frontal s.
Inferior frontal s.
Precentral s.
Central s.
Post central s.
Intraparie
Trans.-parietal s.
NATIONAL MUSEUM OF HEALTH AND MEDICI

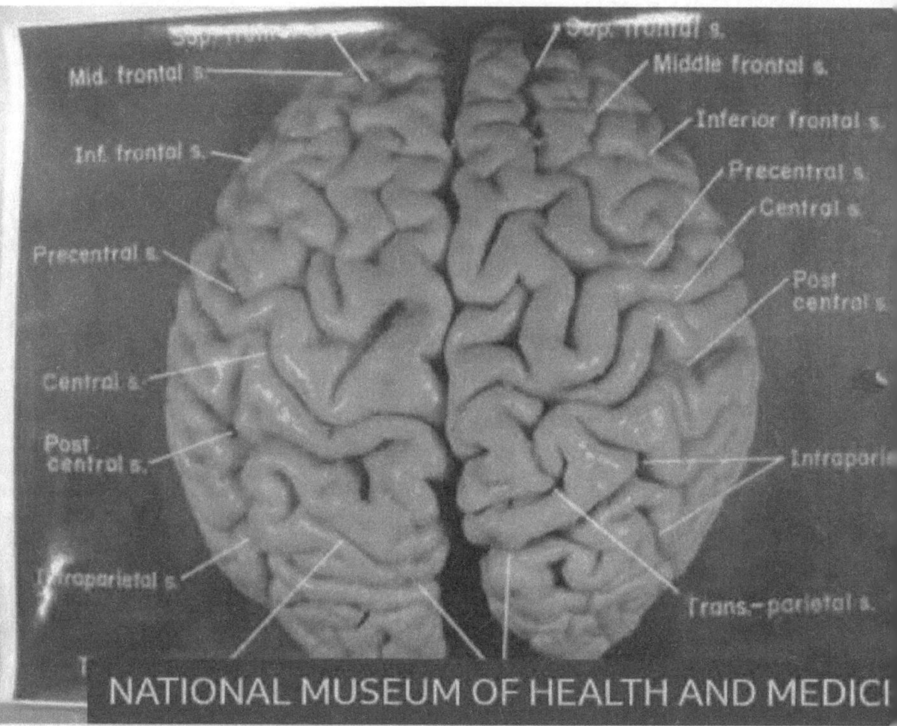

Did a momentous work in 1950
He described the Unified field theory

In 1922 Einstein was awarded Noble prize in physics
For his services in theoretical physics

Nobel "prize money was deposited in Swiss bank
For his wife Mileva Maric

In 1913 he was granted full membership
In Prussian academy of Sciences

Awarded Copley medal by Royal Society
Also awarded the Gold medal of the Royal
Astronomical Society

Max plank presented Einstein with max plank medal
Of The German physical society in Berlin

He received the Prix Jules Jansen
In year 1931

He was awarded the Franklin medal
His statue is in Washington Albert Einstein memorial

The chemical element 99
Was named after Einstein.
In 1999 Time magazine named him Person of
century
Ahead of Roosevelt and MK Gandhi

E=mc2

His name was added to Walhalla Temple
For Germans mainly, distinguished and laudable.

On his name their is a mountain
Called Mount Einstein

Einstein tower - astrophysical Observatory
Built to perform checks on Einstein's General relativity

One of the most brilliant minds in history
Loved to ate fried eggs mushroom and honey

Mutter museum is the place where you can see his brain
20 microns thick and stained.

Thomas Stoltz Harvey
Conducted Einstein's autopsy.

He took the brain anyway
Without permission from his family

He liked to drink Kaffee Haag
And liked celery punch

Only friend of Einstein was Yuri
He was attached with him emotionally

Said to be the best Physicist of 20th centaury
Was having Blood type B'

E=mc2

He was although late talker
But with time became Voracious reader

In April 1955
Einstein went to afterlife.

He was suffering from abdominal aortic aneurysm
And his brain was stolen and kept in museum.

I can't imagine
A world without Einstein

A world with no technology
We wouldn't have best magnets that depend on superconductivity

For starters we wouldn't have GPS
No link between energy and mass.
It would have taken decades to understand gravity
And Energy mass equivalence famously.

He was neither eager to be famous
Nor striving to be great, he was Genius
He enjoyed the Notoriety
Having theorized relativity

The most precious pearl to be found on Earth
Was and is Albert - the man of worth
He received and deserved Nobel Prize
$E= mc^2$ brilliantly clarifies.

Mark the 100th anniversary
Of Einstein's theory of special relativity

E=mc2

It took my enough
To spare an hour to write a rhyme

So let's see
How this equation changed world irrevocably
Will explain the story
Through poetry

Of the famous discovery
$E= mc^2$ wholly

Explains things of sheer wonder
Changed history and Einstein for ever.

E' is the energy in E=mc squared
In Joules it is measured.

M represents mass
That we measure in kilograms.

In equation $E= mc^2$ C
Represents speed of light in vacuity
Anyone Who read books by Isaac Asimov
Speed in Latin is 'celeritas', you must know

Tiny mass can equal big energy
Paper towels, lasers work on relativity.

It is Einstein
Who revolutionized our understanding of space,
time.

E=mc2

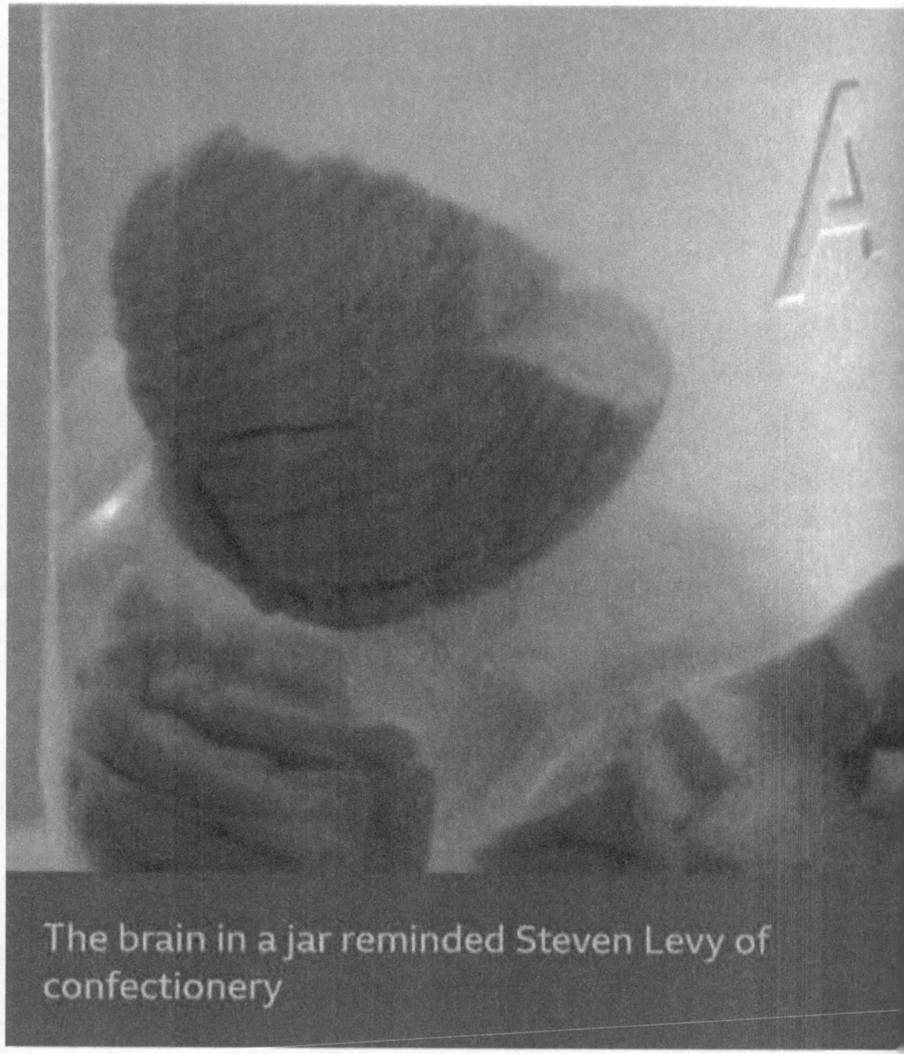

Einstein gave out his famous equation
E=mc squared That transformed this world.

Came to application of public 2nd world war.
When brutal Hitler came into power.
At the time Germany
Was the heart of science and technology.

E= mc^2 was used
And Atom Bomb was produced.

Heisenberg was in the lead of Project
After many tireless hard works they discovered way
of Bombardment.

But this way was bulk
Szilard met Einstein to discuss this topic.

And deduced instead of alpha particles.
They used neutron' newly discovered particles.

Szilard convinced Einstein to tell this project And
wrote letter to us president Roosevelt.
US president ordered this their group of scientist
To start the project which was famous as Manhattan
Project.

Due to this valuable contribution
He was offered American Citizenship

E=mc2

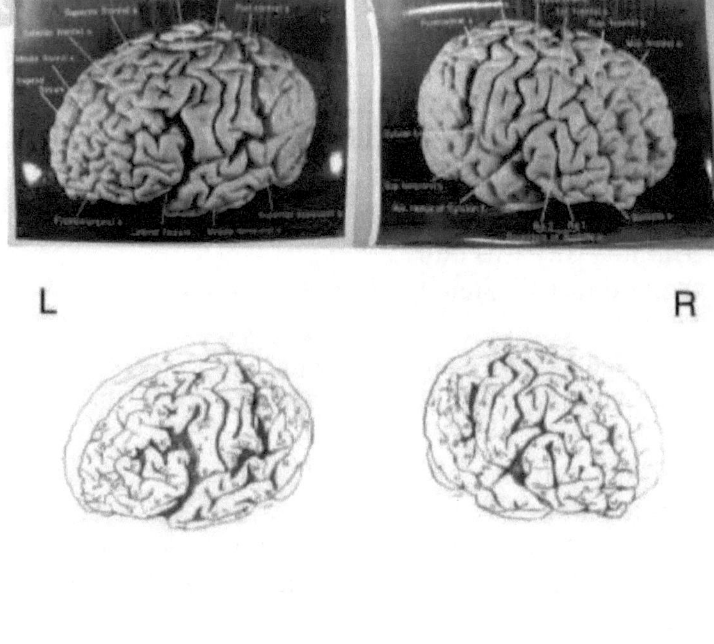

US used correct way now
To produce atom bomb

They were progressing rapidly
Bomb was used prepared to used it **against** Germany

On may 7, 1945
Germany surrendered to Allies.

Instead using it on Germany
They dropped on Hiroshima and Nagasaki

Because
Japan was also enemy of Us.

Although Atom Bomb ended the war
But the result was Scary

The explosion
Resulted in destruction.

Now a days people in those cities mostly
People are unfit physically

Einstein didn't play any role
His Small equation ruined generations of those

Even Einstein couldn't believe the outcome
Of that Atom Bomb.

His equation of hard work
Because equation of death.

E=mc2

Einstein appeared as scientific devil
Nuclear effect proved terrible

Einstein's equation is not Just an equation of destruction
But also an ultimate equation of creation.

Other side of equation tells us
Something else i.e. amount of energy can be
Condensed back to back to mass.

When we drive our car
$E=mc^2$ is at work

Engine burns gasoline produces energy
Here works special relativity.

When we use mP3 player
$E=mc^2$ is that time in power.

From Smoke detectors to exit signs
Work on equation of Einstein.

The production of nuclear power from uranium to plutonium
Relies on this principle.

Atom bomb based on both fusion and fission
Is the result of this equation.

Rovers sent to moon and mars saved by the utilization
Of this very equation

E=mc2

The large Hadron collider
Giant neutrino detector

Tells us about the nature
Universe and matter

Works the utilization
Of this great equation

Our existence: breathing, eating frowning action and
emotion
Is because of this equation.

Remember $E=mc^2$ expresses interchange ability
Between mass and Energy

Equation $E=mc^2$ is wholly mathematical
Archaeologists use to date ancient material.

What we can deduce from equation: E=mc squared
Mass is not conserved.

Nothing is permanent, no laws are fixed
Tells $E=mc^2$ by its charm whole world got beguiled.

Proves everything is relative
Scientific thinking is inductive.

It leads to hydrogen Bomb
Heralded in with drum roll and aplomb.

E=mc2

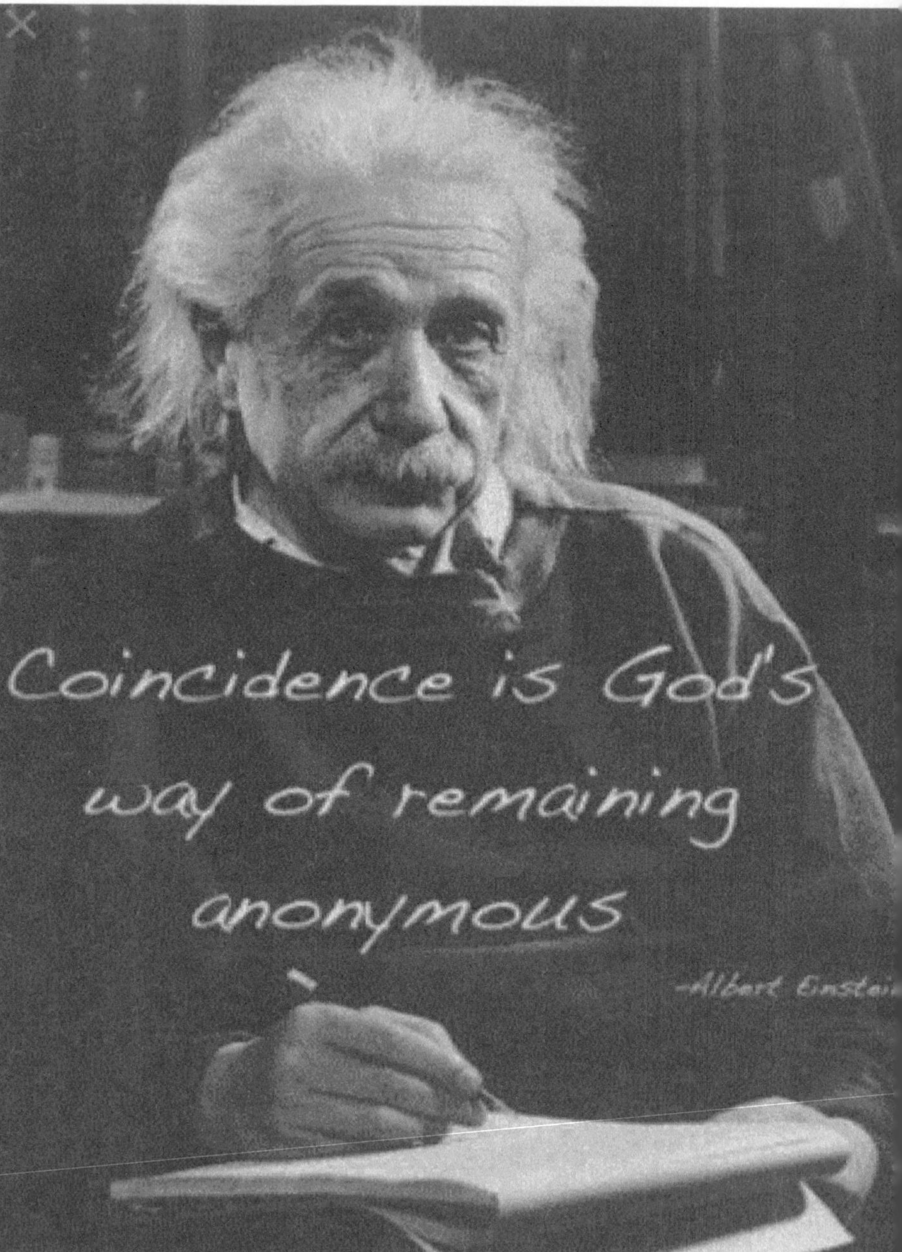

Coincidence is God's
way of remaining
anonymous
-Albert Einstein

He knows inside a small mass
Lies energy, tremendous.

Lulled by laziness of light
He angered light

There he made it
Much energy was released

When we are looking at Stars, Einstein
Says we are looking back in time,

We can create matter directly
Says, Einstein from pure energy

We do it all the time
In Sun, black holes says Einstein

In cosmic catastrophes
In particle accelerators

We are constantly
Creating matter out of energy

Let me give you an example i.e. easy
Take two protons with enough energy

Smash them together
You get 3 Proton one antiproton dear.

Exact process used to take place at Fermi lab
accelerator

E=mc2

NMHMC Harvey Collection - part 181 slide 465 (occipital)
NATIONAL MUSEUM OF HEALTH AND MEDICI

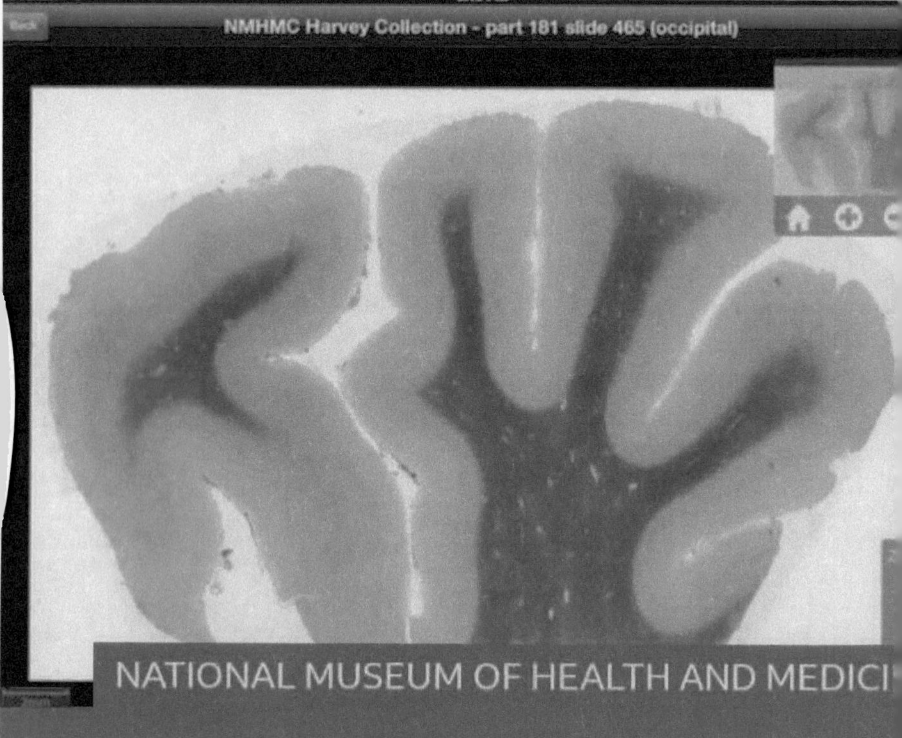

This is how we made vast majority of antimatter.

Mass is Just one form of energy
That can be created that or destroyed easily

More common and even mundane application
Of Einstein most famous equation

When you combust H_2 gas with O2 to make water
It gives off energy, made famous by Hindenburg disaster

When you do something that releases energy, this equation
Tells you are losing mass in direct proportion.

Each time you bat an eyelid breath in or out
Flex a muscle think a thought or beat your heart

You convert mass into energy
Truly, flashy, matching its popularity

Is its deceiving complexity
Its symbol although recognize easily

Embody concepts contrary
To the way things seem to be.

Notation $E=mc^2$ is visually simple
Elegantly meaningful

It is capable of powering the production
Of energy and of causing great devastation.

Albert Einstein's brain was stolen after death for research

After Albert Einstein's death on April 18, 1955, Princeton researcher Thomas Harvey removed his brain without prior permission during autopsy. Einstein's family learned about it the next day from the New York Times but later gave a reluctant approval to conduct research. In 1999, a Canadian study claimed Einstein possessed unusual folds in the brain part associated with mathematical ability.

It has been printed on countless T-shirts
Stared in films, printed on posters.

This equation was in a paper submitted to Amalen
der Physik.
Does the inertia of body depend upon energy content.

Energy and mass are not just mathematically related
They are different ways to measure the same thing

Earth, water, fire, air, ether, mind and false egos
All together these constitute separate material
energies

Nainamchindatisastrani
NainamdahatipavaKani

Na Caiman kledayanti
Apo no Sosayatimarutah

Proves Soul is nothing but energy said by Krishna
Soul can never be cut into pieces by weapon.

Nor can be burned by fire
Nor moistened by water

Nor withered by wind
Just leaves old body and Find new.
Einstein's theory
Explains why mercury is liquid why gold shiny.

Mass became a way to measure total energy present
In any object

Even when it wasn't being heated
Moved or irradiated.

Energy is said to be conserved
Only if you account for changing masses.

Our sun shine
Due to equation of Einstein.

We can create anything
Out of Nothing.

Einstein is justly
Famous for devising his theory

The theory of relativity
Which revolutionize understanding of space, time
and Gravity

It's very vital
For understanding properties of antimatter.

And also tiny
Mass can equal big energy

Equations most far reaching Legacy
Is it provides the key
To understand microscopic activity
Small amount of mass produce large energy

Equivalence of mass-energy also comes in handy
when study antimatter

E=mc2

When particle meets anti-particle, they annihilate
each other Einstein's formula also counts
Heat in our planets crust

Prophet visited hell and paradise at the speed of light
Crossed sidrat-ul-muntaha all in less than night

Angel Gabriel also visited our planet from 7th
heaven many a time
Hence, proves equation of great Einstein

Every single object in universe is Just piece of
immensely compressed energy
That's what tells Einstein's theory of relativity.

Quran says, "A day with your lord is equivalent
To thousand years in the way you count

Angles and spirits ascent to him in a day.
Whose length is thousand years that's what the Quran
does say.

Quran says near Allah there is value of time
Relativity theory of Einstein.

Mass and energy are eternal having
No end, no beginning

This equation is amusing
As well as enticing

We understood power of sun
Equation gave birth to nuclear weapon

E=mc2

Einstein's equations
Showed Time is illusion

Massive objects cause distortion in space-time
Felt as Gravity tells Einstein

When an object approaches speed of light
Mass becomes infinite

Clocks on airplanes and satellite Travels
At different speed, tells Einstein.

Let's thank Einstein for thinking
Outside the box'.

He was faster than horse
And his endurance greater than ox

He was a rare genius
And $E=mc^2$ was ingenious

It is Einstein.
Who transformed our vision of space and time

His discoveries really did enable a wide array of
Technology
News articles often put Einstein's IQ at 160
$E=mc^2$: A road from here
Leads there

In a dream world everything is possible.
Laws are admissible.

E=mc2

E=mc^2: We are at bidirectional road choice is there.
You quiet, move forward backward, Beware

All roads lead us to where?

***